# THE House Next Door

# THE House Next Door

## SEATTLE'S NEIGHBORHOOD ARCHITECTURE   by Lila Gault

Photography by Mary Randlett

Pacific Search Press

Pacific Search Press
      222 Dexter Avenue North, Seattle, Washington  98109
© 1981 text by Lila Gault
© 1981 photographs by Mary Randlett. All rights reserved
Printed in the United States of America

Designed by Judy Petry

**Library of Congress Cataloging in Publication Data**

Gault, Lila.
      The house next door.

      Bibliography: p.
      1. Seattle (Wash.)—Dwellings. 2. Architecture,
Domestic—Washington (State)—Seattle. 3. Ver-
nacular architecture—Washington (State)—Seattle.
I. Title.
NA 7238.S4G3      728.3′7′0979777      81-38375
ISBN 0-914718-61-4                        AACR2

*To Mac, who taught me that a house is more than just shelter*

# Contents

*We are grateful to those people who let us explore their houses and to others who supported us in innumerable ways while we worked.*

Jane Adams

Lee and Carol Bassett

Phillip Blumstein

Marion Boyer

Al Bumgardner

Terri DeMierre

Gary and Cindy Donion

Dana Dwinnell and Ken Rose

Margaret Enderlein

Mike and Sobie Fortman

Paul Gillingham

Tim Howland

Jennifer James

Steve Johnson

Hans Jorgensen

Bob Kaplan

Kathy Kirkwood

Wendy Kneedler and
  Geoffrey Senior

Betsy and Bill Lawrence

Earl Layman

Dennis Mortensen

John Owen

Mark Peckham

Kate Pflaumer

Fred Repass

Pepper Schwartz

Gary and Jennifer Sortun

Hugh Stratford

Nancy Tobie

Mark Von Walter

Bill and Suellen Wigen

Elizabeth Bayley Willis

Virginia Clarke Younger

# The Growth of a Livable City: Seattle from 1900 to 1930

No single element of a cityscape describes the fundamental growth and quality of urban life as well as an architectural profile of a typical residential community. We can tell just how prosperous, imaginative, status-conscious, and resourceful the city's residents were, and still are, by strolling through a few characteristic neighborhoods. The dwellings that were and are being built, whether they are single-family houses, duplexes, or high-rise apartments, give us a vivid visual picture of the growth of a city in both past and present tense.

When we look at a typical residential neighborhood in Seattle, the relative prosperity of its citizens and the abundant supply of available land become apparent by the overwhelming popularity of the single-family house. From Beacon Hill to Ballard and from Magnolia to Laurelhurst, Seattle is a city of houses, only occasionally punctuated by apartment buildings and other multiple units.

Seattle's existing housing stock has finally been recognized as a significant, irreplaceable urban resource by both citizens and planners. The demand for convenient, affordable housing has prompted thousands of prospective homeowners to return to, or remain in, the city. As a result, virtually every neighborhood within minutes of the downtown business core has undergone a dramatic renaissance in the past ten years.

Prospective owners usually are interested in more than just a convenient bargain per square foot when they buy and renovate an older Seattle house. Many of the city's modest, so-called popular houses, especially those built between 1890 and 1930, offer interesting or significant architectural design, lavish use of quality materials, especially in interiors, and remarkable finish craftsmanship.

Although Seattle contains a respectable number of mansions for a city of half a million, it certainly is not recognized as a city of "great houses." Nor is the architectural profile dominated by a particular style, such as the brownstone townhouses of New York or the Victorian residences of San Francisco. Instead, Seattle's vernacular housing reflects the moods of its craftsmen, the whims of local developers, and the prosperity of its residents.

Stylistically, the variety of Seattle's popular housing reflects the fashions in residential design that swept the country from coast to coast between 1890 and 1930. Most of these styles—including Victorian, Craftsman, and Tudor—came west; but others, particularly the bungalow and Spanish Mission, arrived in Seattle from California before moving east.

Although many of Seattle's ordinary houses were built in a pure and certain style, many combined elements of several styles, or perhaps more typically, showed no particular style at all and were known simply as "builder" houses. The builder house was designed and constructed by the same hand, often from purchased plans but sometimes simply from successful experience with satisfied buyers.

Much of the vernacular housing in Seattle is characterized by a certain eclectic quality. On any typical block between Mount Baker and Ballard, one finds half a dozen different styles, each one different from the house next door. Although some of these houses have views of mountains and water, most simply look onto the house across the street. A few are located on double or corner lots, but most sit on a standard fifty-by-one-hundred foot parcel.

Seattle's popular houses were built by thousands of builders who were either employed by a prospective owner for a certain lot or who worked on a speculative basis for themselves or a developer. Most worked from various catalogs of stock plans published by architects such as Seattle's Judd Yoho. Yoho, who also published the monthly *Bungalow Magazine* from 1913 to 1918, published several editions of *The Bungalow Craftsman,* a catalog that offered dozens of different plans in the popular bungalow style. Plans and specifications could be obtained from the architect for five dollars. Since Yoho advertised his custom work at five dollars per room, a catalog plan saved both builder and owner a substantial sum.

The builder would often modify a plan to suit a client's special needs. Progress and quality of construction depended entirely on the builder. Some builders, especially those who specialized in finish work, were craftsmen, but many were not. The introduction of building codes eliminated some of the sloppiest work in later years, but in the early days the builder was totally responsible for quality control. As a result, all of Seattle's neighborhood houses were not well built, as many a sagging floor dramatically attests.

Despite variations in the quality of construction, good

materials were generally used in these houses, especially those built before 1930. Lumber mills within a few miles of almost every building site turned out framing and finish boards in inexpensive abundance. Hardwoods, such as Siberian oak and maple, were also in good supply and frequently used for finish flooring. Decorative leaded windows were often stopped into exterior walls for ornamentation, as well as used for door panels on book-cases, breakfronts, and other built-in cabinetry.

Brass was the common material for door and window hardware, switch plates, and light fixtures. And although the fancy turnings and trim of the high Victorian era were never commonly found in Seattle, local millworkers produced fancy doors and intricate moldings for interiors, and turned spindles and newels for stair railings.

The generally high quality and great quantity of Seattle's neighborhood houses can be explained in many ways. Probably most important was the slow, steady growth of the city, which minimized the demand for wholesale speculative building. In addition, the financial comfort of most of the city's working residents allowed many homeowners to ornament an otherwise modest house with handsome finish detail and to borrow certain design elements from concurrent residential architecture for the rich. Finally, the variety of recreational oppor-tunities and amenities scattered over a wide geographical area surrounding the central city attracted potential homeowners to residential areas nearby.

Seventeen different residences, located in neighbor-hoods from Mount Baker to Ravenna and from Queen Anne to Ballard, are described in this book. The oldest was built in 1900; the most recent in 1928. Although the two decades before the turn of the century and the years since 1930 have seen some historic and architecturally significant residential design, it was in the first three decades of this century that the city's neighborhood architecture really flourished.

Some of these houses have simply been painted and papered occasionally throughout the years; others have undergone minor structural alterations to suit requirements of new owners. Several have had their functional living space substantially increased by finishing the attic or basement, and a few have experienced almost complete interior renovation. Regardless of interior treatment, each house has retained its original exterior character and, in most cases, its original appearance from the street.

These particular houses represent more than just the dedication, good taste, and creativity of their owners; they also represent a valuable and appreciated urban resource—the existing housing stock of a vital, thriving city.

# The Houses

# 1900 WALLINGFORD

At first glance this sturdy, somewhat plain one-and-a-half story house, located in the Wallingford district just a few blocks from Lower Woodland Park, appears to be in original turn-of-the-century condition, lovingly maintained by a handful of dedicated and thoughtful owners through the years. In fact, just five years ago, the house was a dilapidated rental, owned and largely ignored by an immediate neighbor. When the current owners made an offer to buy the house, the landlord was happy to sell.

The current owners paid $20,000 in 1974 for the neglected structure and its attractive site, a standard fifty-by-one-hundred foot lot that seems larger because of its corner location. The house, conveniently located within walking distance of a park, stores, and schools, had some obvious architectural character despite several careless remodeling attempts. Most importantly, it was affordable. It would take five years of nights, weekends, and vacations, plus about as much cash as the purchase price, to bring the house to its present handsome and comfortable state.

The house was originally built on a lot four blocks away and moved to its present location about ten years later. Its structural condition remained sound, especially for a typical builder house of that day. But during a 1950s style remodeling the owners replaced most of the wood sash window frames with aluminum, lowered the ceiling in the kitchen, and installed "modern" fixtures in the bathroom. In addition, the original wiring was inadequate, plaster walls were waterstained and badly cracked, and almost all of the original interior trim had been painted several times. The exterior had been modernized with the addition of a small porch over the front door and an asymmetrical extension of the overhead gable, dramatically altering the original roofline.

From the outset, the owners planned to do most of the design and construction themselves. They spent months walking around their neighborhood and others of similar vintage looking for houses like their own, and spent hours searching for ideas in the library and at bookstores.

13

14

To restore the facade to its original roofline and add some stylish character to a plain and simple house, they removed the existing porch and returned the gable to its symmetrical dimensions. They built a veranda, adorned with a decorative railing of fancy spindles and posts, across the front of the house; completely repainted the exterior; and replaced portions of the composition shingle roof.

To create privacy from their neighbors and the street, the owners planted a dense hedge of laurel along the western property line and built a fence around the backyard. The shrubbery grew rapidly to eye level and now blends attractively with the fence to form an effective screen.

While the exterior was being restored and enhanced, the interior was being renovated as well. Hardwood floors in the entry, parlor, and dining room were professionally refinished. Then the owners went to work on the stairs, stripping layers of paint from spindles, newels, railings, and trim. The tedious process of stripping painted woodwork was relieved by the creative work of building the front door, which features a colorful stained-glass panel as well as several sets of wooden windows.

15

Almost all of the original light fixtures, hardware, and fittings had disappeared long before the current owners took possession of the house. They installed antique brass switch plates, light globes salvaged from a condemned Granite Falls schoolhouse, and even a brass mail slot. The interior is still being renovated, room by room, with attractive finish details to be added after new wiring and wallboard have been installed.

The bathroom and the smallest of the three bedrooms upstairs were brightened with new walls to replace water-damaged original plaster, new paint, and handsome, well-built cabinetry. The small bathroom was designed to provide maximum storage with a handcrafted oak vanity, wall cabinets, and a ship-style ladder to hold towels. The bedroom also functions efficiently with the addition of a floor-to-ceiling wall unit, designed and built by the owner, which serves as a dresser, closet, and small desk for a growing son.

Although the owners planned to make as few changes in the original floor plan as possible, they did agree that the kitchen would have to be enlarged, offer more storage and food preparation surface, and admit more natural light. In addition, they desired an informal eating area.

To make efficient use of existing floor space, the owners enclosed the back porch and built large windows into the new outside wall to allow maximum use of natural light. A breakfast bar was built at one end of the former porch area, and cabinets were built into the other end, just inside the door to the backyard. The eating area now faces the kitchen, where plastic laminate and oak-trimmed cabinets have been installed on three walls. A band of glass-front cabinets at the top serves primarily as convenient display for a collection of attractive stoneware.

The kitchen has become the activity center of the house, in part because the owners like to cook, but also because the room is light and spacious. Perhaps its greatest attraction is the large tinned panel on the ten-foot ceiling, uncovered unexpectedly by the owners during the remodeling. Panels such as this one were often installed in turn-of-the-century kitchens to protect the rest of the house from fire. This panel has been painted with a glossy blue-gray enamel that blends easily with the soft creams and browns of the kitchen cabinets, countertops, and floor, yet enhances the distinctive texture of the panel's embossed surface.

# 1901 CAPITOL HILL

"Although I certainly enjoy the panoramic view from virtually any room on the west side of the house," said the owner-architect of this handsomely renovated Capitol Hill house, "I really was attracted to the place by the opportunity to design and build a private courtyard on the other side between the house and the street. In addition, the price was fair, the location convenient, and the size adequate for both an office and a residence. So I bought the house in 1957, planning to renovate it for long-term use as an office and only brief use as a residence. Twenty-three years later, the office has moved to larger quarters and I'm still living in the house."

The gambrel roof dominates the exterior massing of this Dutch Colonial builder house, built in 1901 on the west slope of Capitol Hill just below some of Seattle's finest houses. The owner did all the design work and much of the construction in the early stages of the renovation. Although much of the house has been redesigned and rebuilt, it now reflects its modest origins—a simple interior plan and functional use of limited space.

"I believe that a house should be adapted to the needs of its owners and should be designed in a way that allows for change as different situations develop," the owner emphasized as he described the work on the house. He devised the renovation process to proceed in three separate stages, focusing one at a time on specific areas, or zones, in the house. Since the limitations of time and money did not permit him to complete the entire job at once, he evaluated his needs in order of importance, and then went to work.

A small porch that provided shelter just in front of the front door was removed and the main entry relocated on the side of the house. The owner then could create a much-

desired courtyard, surrounded by a high fence and a dense planting of shrubbery and trees. This very private outdoor location serves as an entertaining area for large parties, as well as a quiet dining room for a gathering of a few friends.

The relocation of the main entry of the house, from the front to the side, rearranged the interior plan as well. The new front door opened into a somewhat large entry with a conference room to one side. When his office was located in the house, the owner used the entry as a reception area. Now it is a repository for handsome antique furnishings, and a collection of books, ceramics, and games housed on built-in shelves along one wall.

In the second phase of renovation, the owner redesigned the kitchen and informal eating area and integrated this interior space with the courtyard just outside. Leaded windows, salvaged from a nearby house that was demolished because of the freeway, were used in the outside wall to open the courtyard view to the kitchen and to allow as much natural light as possible to enter the house on that side.

The stairwell to the second floor was opened to the roofline to create a dramatic vertical space. The pipe rising from a small tiled stove and the parallel furnace flue accentuate the vertical emphasis, which creates a spacious feeling in this area.

On the second floor, the final phase of renovation was completed by replacing three small bedrooms and a bath with a spacious master suite, divided into sleeping and sitting areas, and a completely remodeled bath. Original flat ceilings were removed to expose the slope of the roof, and beveled redwood siding was installed. The angular roofline is also revealed in one wall of the tiled shower. A small bay window lets natural light into the suite from the south, as does a prow window on the east side, but the room focuses on the windows that frame the expansive view of Queen Anne Hill and beyond to the west.

The first floor boasts original hardwood floors, which have been oiled and polished to create a rich patina. That flooring was the only quality material in the original house, the owner pointed out, adding that there was no trim or molding of any practical or aesthetic value. Woven fiber matting covers the patched-together fir floorboards on the second floor and the treads on the stairs.

Although the major renovation was completed years ago, work on this 1700-square-foot house continues as the need arises. When the house became strictly a residence several years ago, the owner decided to remodel the basement into a rental apartment. To hide the location of the former stairs to the basement, he installed a prefabricated firebox in the living room. When he decided to use the foyer to grow large houseplants, he had a large skylight cut into the roof to permit additional natural light to reach this previously dark area.

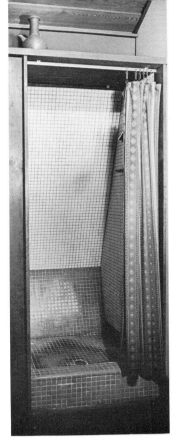

# 1903 CAPITOL HILL

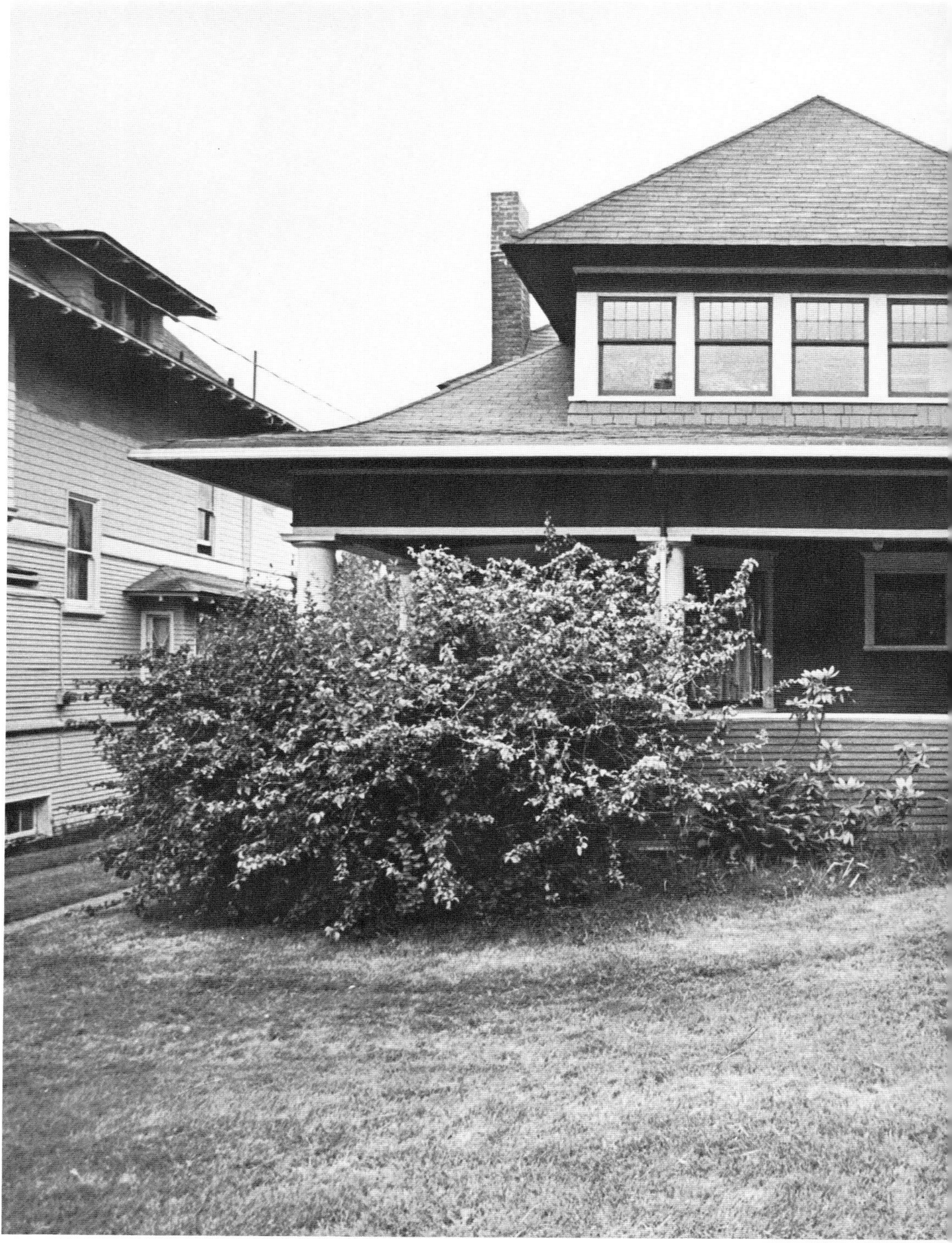

Although certain residential architectural styles were widely popular on Capitol Hill in 1903 when this house was built, dwellings that combined a variety of stylistic elements were not uncommon. This residence, virtually unchanged since its completion nearly eighty years ago, is a remarkable example of eclectic design characteristics.

The one-and-a-half story elevation beneath a sloping gable roof suggests a bungalow, but that particular style had barely arrived in Seattle in 1903. The wide overhangs of the roof, which give the house a decidedly horizontal profile from the street, suggest the then current Prairie style of Frank Lloyd Wright, while the distinctive semicircular bay window and large pillars that support the roof over the portico are reminiscent of more classical ornamentation.

While many residential blocks in the emerging neighborhoods around the city included a dozen copies of the same basic style, other blocks, such as the one adjacent to Volunteer Park where this frame residence is located, boast half a dozen different styles on the same side of the street. Although stylistic variety among houses was commonly found on a single block, few individual structures demonstrate a remarkable combination of design elements as dramatically as this house.

The interior of this comfortable, three-bedroom dwelling offers a number of interesting finish details. The built-in bench opposite the front door in the large entry is borrowed from the Craftsman style, in which built-in furnishings were an essential element. The entry is separated from the adjacent living room by a pair of sliding pocket doors, which still boast their original brass hardware.

The living room is accented by a large bay window at one end, but the focus of activity is a large fireplace, faced with unusual jade-green tile. A second pair of pocket doors can be closed to separate the living room from the large, formal dining room. Large double-hung windows on two walls in the dining room admit plentiful natural light.

Even the kitchen remains much as it was when built in 1903. New linoleum flooring has been laid over the original fir floor, however, and the cabinet doors were removed by previous owners to create an open-shelf system of storage. Maple counter-tops, well seasoned after years of use and varnished to prevent deterioration, add a warm richness to this bright room. A small pantry between the kitchen and dining room has been converted into an informal breakfast area.

Oak flooring in the entry, living room, and dining room has been refinished in rich dark tones and blends handsomely with the finish trim that frames all of the windows and doors. Many of the original brass light fixtures, switch plates, door knobs, and other hard-ware are still in place and are enhanced by the dark floor and finish trim.

Each of the three bedrooms on the second floor has a large walk-in closet and coved ceilings. There is a view of the Olympics from the bedroom at the back of the house. In front, a sun porch fills the gable end that faces the street and serves as an ideal location for thriving houseplants. French doors separate the sun porch from an adjacent bedroom; together, the porch and bedroom make a comfortable and spacious suite.

Even the bathroom in this house has survived years of use in remarkably good condition. One-inch white hexagonal tile covers the floor, the walls of a large walk-in shower stall, and the bathtub backsplash. A pedestal sink remains in use, as does the original toilet.

# 1903 CAPITOL HILL

"I like the coziness of this small house," remarked the owner of this builder cottage located on a quiet street in north Capitol Hill. "It's a comfortable size for one or two, with ample space for almost everything except entertaining a crowd of people. I felt that I could live in this house and be myself without making too many changes that would alter its charm and character."

When she first moved to Seattle three years ago, she purchased the house because of its size, convenient location, and landscaped seclusion from neighboring houses and the street. In addition, the modest and unassuming facade and interior provided a perfect opportunity for her own decoration and design ideas.

Small, somewhat styleless cottages of this type were built throughout the city after the turn of the century, often as quick speculative ventures by a builder. These frame houses were simple—a small square plan beneath a hip roof with minimal ornamentation.

This particular house is typical. Ornamentation is limited to raised medallions on the outside of the entry door and a panel of leaded glass in the central section of the living room and dining room bay windows. A small porch adds interest at the entry.

The simple floor plan is divided almost equally into sleeping rooms and common rooms. The living room and dining room are really one large room; the owner has established their separate functions with a large handpainted screen. The kitchen, located next to the dining room, is also accessible from the backyard through a tiny pantry and mud room. Each of the rooms in the house, including the two

bedrooms, has a ten-foot ceiling, which gives a deceptively spacious quality to this 800-square-foot house. Storage on the main floor is limited to two large closets, but there is a large basement, a small attic, and a separate, full-sized garage.

The owner, whose professional life is devoted to a family-owned home-furnishing showroom, has chosen fabrics and papers in muted tones to cover the walls in the living and dining rooms, as well as in the bedrooms. She removed wall-to-wall carpeting and had the oak flooring refinished in the living and dining rooms. Since the remaining flooring was unattractive fir, the entry, kitchen, and bedroom floors were covered with terra-cotta Mexican pavers, an earthtone hexagonal tile that gives a contemporary look and still seems to harmonize with the vintage character of the rest of the house.

Originally, the house was heated with a coal-fired stove vented through a chimney in the kitchen; currently a gas furnace provides heat. The owner added a fireplace in the living room, but did so in such a way that from both inside and out, the installation seems original. The other major structural change in the house was the addition of a small deck across the back, with a pair of French doors installed in the rear bedroom wall to provide access.

The owner has enhanced the charming character and basic comfort of this seventy-seven-year-old house by adapting the original plan to suit her own needs—adding a deck and living room fireplace, and using her design experience to update and brighten the interior.

# 1906 CAPITOL HILL

The Seattle classic box has a unique distinction among residential architectural styles because it was first recognized and identified as a housing style by two Seattle architectural historians. The Seattle classic box was the preferred house for the upwardly mobile in the city during the first decade of this century. As a result, hundreds of these houses—from fancy to plain—can be found in neighborhoods from Mount Baker to the University District.

The style is most prevalent, however, at the top of Capitol Hill, south and east of Volunteer Park. Several entire blocks are built entirely of Seattle classic boxes, whose basic two-story plan measures thirty-two by thirty-six feet topped by an almost flat hip roof. The entry is always located at the left or the right on the first floor of the facade (never in the center as in many housing styles) and is often adorned with a covered porch supported by columns or pillars.

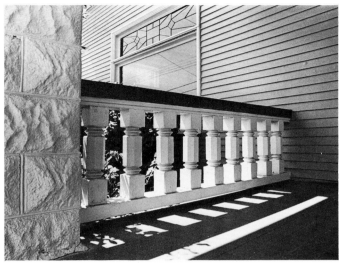

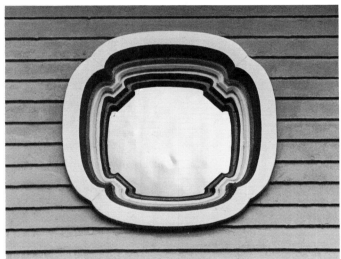

The term classic box is inspired by the boxlike shape of the dwelling, as well as by the classic ornamentation that often appears on the facade. As with all of Seattle's popular housing styles, the extent of decoration and finish detail depended on the owner's or developer's budget. Many Seattle classic boxes evidence elaborate ornamentation; typically, most have at least a small decorative window in the center of the facade that faces the street.

The standard floor plan of the classic box featured four spacious common rooms on the first floor, and four large bedrooms and a bathroom on the second level. A large entry inside the front door allowed the owner to greet guests in a formal setting. The living room, dominated by a large fireplace, was located next to the entry. These two rooms were often separated by sliding doors. The dining room, usually somewhat larger than the living room, was located between the living room and the kitchen. An enclosed porch was often attached to the first floor at the back of the house and could be reached through the kitchen or from the backyard. Four bedrooms of equal size and a bathroom were usually located on the second floor. Each corner bedroom window was built as an extended bay, which provided a window seat inside and a distinctive appearance outside.

43

One such house, located several blocks from Volunteer Park, has been lovingly renovated by its owners in the past four years, as have many other classic boxes in the neighborhood. This particular example is neither the plainest nor the fanciest and gives a typical view of this distinctive style.

Once occupied by an owner of some means, this house, like many others in the neighborhood, became a rooming house for a number of years. As a result, when the current owners took possession, the house had been adapted for use by five or six unrelated occupants, had undergone some structural alterations, and suffered from the lack of regular maintenance.

They replaced cracked plaster walls with wall-board, rewired, and removed temporary partitions from some of the rooms. The kitchen was relocated on the former back porch, new appliances were installed, and walls and cabinets were repainted. Fir flooring in the kitchen was refinished, as was the quarter-sawn oak flooring in the living and dining rooms.

Although much of the original hardware had disappeared, the owners did find a handsome ceiling light fixture still in place in the dining room. Perhaps the most valuable ornamentation also survived years of indifferent owners and careless tenants. The upper panel of almost every double hung window is beveled-zinced glass; decorative panels also are found elsewhere.

1908 MADRONA

Certain vintage houses, especially those showing little or no architectural character, are best adapted for current use by careful remodeling. Such is the case with this standard builder cottage, which was originally built as a summer cabin near Lake Washington, in the Madrona district. Attracted to its location and modest price of $19,000, the current owner bought the house in 1974. He then hired a designer-builder to help renovate the modest structure to suit his needs.

The owner had two specific goals in mind for remodeling the structure. First, he wanted to eliminate the cramped feeling in the small, separately enclosed living and dining rooms. Second, he wanted to renovate a badly deteriorated bathroom, located just off the master bedroom.

The living and dining rooms were combined into a large single area by removing an existing wall between them. The two areas continue to serve separate functions, divided visually by a large fireplace and chimney. The elimina-tion of a small hallway that went from the front door back to the kitchen allowed additional floor space to be included in the new living-dining area and also made wall space available for built-in bookshelves and stereo storage.

The bathroom was gutted and then paneled with rough-cut cedar. Prussian blue tile was installed in the shower and on the vanity countertop. A square stained-glass panel with accents of gold on a blue background was installed in the existing window frame to provide privacy from the street.

Once a plain and modestly finished cottage, the house now has some striking finish details, including the tile and wood mantel over the fireplace, and the ceiling supports that have replaced the original bearing wall between the former living and dining rooms and attractively frame the cement brick chimney. Original details, such as the wall of windows and French doors that admits maximum light into the redesigned living-dining area, have become more prominent than in the original plan.

Few changes have been made in the original compact kitchen. A small pantry was eliminated to create more workable space. The doors on the existing upper cabinets were removed to allow accessible display of tableware and glasses. The open-shelf design for storage is complemented by several rows of colorful plastic bins and baskets

mounted on another wall.

The lower kitchen cabinets were painted in bright enamel tones and new hardware was installed on the doors and drawers. The original gas stove, which the owner considered replacing when he first saw it, has proved an excellent tool for culinary success, as well as being economical and efficient.

While the carpenters were at work inside the house, the owner and friends went to work outside. Existing shingled sidewalls were painted chocolate brown and a new cedar shingle roof and cedar gutters were installed. The steeply sloping backyard, filled with fruit trees, evergreens, and other valuable plantings, was rescued from the consequences of years of neglect.

Blackberry canes and other brambles were removed, trees and bushes were pruned, and a multi-level system of decks was built. A tall cedar fence was erected for privacy and the garage, located along the alley at the back of the lot, was cleaned up for use as a storage area.

Pleased with the success of the first remodeling effort, the owner is currently making plans to add a breakfast room–solarium adjacent to the kitchen.

51

1910 MADRONA

The late nineteenth-century protest against machine-age artificiality, known in England as the Arts and Crafts Movement, evolved in America into the popular Craftsman, or Mission, style of architecture and furnishings. The Craftsman style was commonly used from 1900 to 1920 by Seattle builders and architects, who took philosophical inspiration and design ideas from the pages of Gustav Stickley's magazine, *The Craftsman,* published in Eastwood, New York, from 1901 to 1916.

The Craftsman style emphasized the use of natural materials, especially wood and stone, to produce a handcrafted look. Elements of this style are commonly found in other popular building types of the period. Rock columns on a bungalow porch, exposed columns and beams, and shingle sidewalls on an otherwise ordinary builder house are all evidence of this popular style.

The interior of a typical Craftsman-style house features maximum use of wood trim and paneling. The functional character of built-in cupboards, book-cases, and seating alcoves also demonstrates the simple, practical principles of the style.

An excellent example of the Craftsman style in Seattle is a two-story builder house built in 1910 in the Madrona district. The current owner bought the house in 1972, in part because of its lavish use of natural materials and quality finish, and also because of its convenient location and spectacular view of Lake Washington and the Cascades.

The roof slopes sharply and is interrupted by two large dormers on opposite sides. The sidewalls are shingled and stained dark brown. An ample porch, tucked underneath the over-hanging gable end, covers the front of the house. The rich, warm quality of this house's facade is carried into the interior by the extensive use of wood in exposed beams, wainscotting, and trim.

The house had been remodeled by previous owners in a way that accentuated its Craftsman character, especially in the living room. The current owner, eager for more space and the privacy of a master suite, renovated the third floor attic into a large, comfortable suite that is in harmony with the original Craftsman finish work on the two floors below.

Part of the living room ceiling was eliminated between the first and second floors, creating a spacious vertical dimension in the main sitting area. More important, it allowed the installation of a large stained-glass window in the south wall to provide a badly needed source of natural light.

A small balcony was built along the upper wall to permit access to a wall the owner uses as a gallery. A railing using post-and-peg detail was built along the balcony, and the railing on the original stairway was removed. The original landing was enlarged and now serves as a hallway to the two bedrooms and small bath on the second floor.

The previous owners not only made structural changes, but also returned the house to its original Craftsman-style appearance by stripping layers of paint from all of the fir trim, wainscotting, and exposed beams, then refinishing the natural surfaces. They even commissioned an appropriately styled light fixture to be handcrafted and installed in the dining room ceiling.

The current owner wanted to renovate the attic the moment she first saw the house, but it took several years before the project actually began. She wanted a bath, bedroom, and study complex built into the existing area and finished with a lot of wood. Her architect used the existing dormers to provide opposing bath and sleeping areas and built a partial wall in front of the tiled bath alcove, thus providing a convenient location for the lavatory and vanity and creating visual privacy for the bath and shower area. A built-in bed faces the view of the lake and a small balcony gives outdoor access to the dramatic panorama. The suite also includes built-in dressers and a desk, and a comfortable sitting area around a freestanding brass firebox.

The cedar-paneled ceiling and oak cabinetry add a rich Craftsman-style look to the suite, which is elegantly complemented by the blue tile in the bath, a stained-glass triptych in the wall behind the whirlpool bathtub, and the wrapped, exposed beams throughout the suite's central core. Skylights cut into the existing roof admit maximum natural light, as do large windows on the south wall.

57

The kitchen also was renovated and now includes a breakfast area, which offers access to the first floor deck. The floor was covered with quarry tile and the ceiling with cedar paneling. Oak countertops were extended to provide more work space and a built-in cupboard installed to display cookbooks and attractive culinary tools.

# 1911 LESCHI

The streetcar ran out to Leschi from downtown Seattle by the turn of the century and brought residents from throughout the city to the district's lakeside beaches and parks. Leschi had been designated a recreation area by the Olmsted brothers in their 1903 plan for Seattle's parks and boulevards, and was already in use when a residential plat of the district was drawn. Steep and often irregular lots were laid out on the bluffs that rose from Lake Washington. Each lot was planned so that, when developed, the house on it would have a panoramic view of the lake and distant mountains, or a more intimate territorial vista of the dense deciduous forest that covered the sloping terrain.

This one-and-a-half story standard builder house was immensely attractive to its current owner, who purchased the house in 1970 because of its expansive view and its double lot. The frame structure was rather ordinary and dull but seemed to offer potential for skillful remodeling. In the meantime, she could pursue her favorite hobby, gardening, in the large yard.

The first alteration was a high fence the owner installed along the front of the house for privacy from neighbors and the street. Then she hired an architect to redesign four small, separate rooms that comprised the main living area into one functional, continuous space. Walls were replaced with graceful arches, and the area was divided into three conversation centers with couches and chairs. The dining room, which has ample storage space in built-in corner cupboards and a large sideboard, is visually, as well as practically, accessible from each of the three sitting areas.

The existing cabinets in the kitchen were repainted, as were the walls and ceiling. New appliances were purchased and installed, and a small table was brought in and placed under a large window to provide a sunny informal breakfast area.

Several years later a major renovation of the second floor was begun. Three small bedrooms and a bath were transformed into two comfortable bedrooms, a conservatory for plants and birds, and two large bathrooms. Actually, the plan functions as two separate suites, one for the owner, the other for her teenage son, with the conservatory a shared area.

The existing master bedroom was retained, and a bathroom was created by combining an adjoining closet with another closet from the smaller bedroom. A whirlpool bathtub was installed and a glass door cut into the east wall behind the tub. A small deck, with a solid wall at one end for privacy, was added outside the glass door. Extensive oak cabinetry in the bathroom adds an elegant touch, and provides convenient storage for towels and bath items.

Quarry tile was laid on the floor of the upstairs level and extended into the entry below. The second bedroom has use of a bathroom across the large central landing, bisected by an exposed chimney coming up from the fireplace below. The built-in desk behind the chimney is used by the student son; a bed built underneath the windows is used by occasional overnight guests.

The conservatory, with a small deck beyond, is a bright haven for birds and indoor plants. Wicker furnishings allow it to be used as a sitting area also. Glass-paneled bifold doors remain open much of the time but can be closed so the plants can be misted and the birds can fly freely around the room.

The exterior has been softened by cedar shingles, which now hide the original frame siding. Aluminum windows, installed in a 1950s modernization, are trimmed with wood on the outside to mask the thin metal frames. A deck just outside the living room connects the house to a hot tub, a greenhouse is attached at ground level to one corner of the house, and at the other corner is a lath house, used to shade indoor plants that spend the summer months outside.

1912 BALLARD

In the late 1890s, Ballard was a town of 2,500 people, most of whom were employed at the Stimson Timber Mill. Many millworkers lived in company cottages, the plain three-room, single-story houses that were built and owned by "the company." Early Ballard houses were typically simple, and even austere, compared with houses in nearby Seattle neighborhoods.

As Ballard expanded with the great influx of immigrants from Sweden, Norway, and Denmark, it became a fishing port and a diversified commercial center. Although it has been assimilated geographically and politically by Seattle, Ballard retains much of its ethnic identity and character. Its housing stock is some of the most well-constructed, if some of the plainest, in the city today and often brings a fair price for both buyer and seller.

This two-story builder house, built in 1912, is a typical well-built Ballard house, and offers handsome exterior ornamentation. Exterior finishing details inspired by the Craftsman style—from the brackets that support the overhanging gable ends to the decoratively milled rafter ends along the sides of the roof and porch overhang—give this house a handcrafted appearance. An element of Victorian ornamentation can be seen in the fancy-cut shingles on the gable end that faces the street.

The current owners liked the stylish character of the house, as well as its modest selling price, and moved in five years ago. Although the house had been neglected, it had not been badly abused. It would take months of stripping and refinishing woodwork and gallons of paint to restore the interior satisfactorily. With an exterior coat of paint and a new roof, the house with its original floor plan would suit the owners very well.

Once they began to live in the house, however, they began to consider some major alterations in the original plan. There was only one bathroom in the entire house, inconveniently located off the kitchen, and four very small bedrooms on the second floor. They decided to create a master suite by converting one of the bedrooms into an upstairs bath. By repositioning some of the walls a large bedroom was created with a good-sized bath adjoining. A skylight was cut into the roof and plumbing brought up through the walls from the first floor bath. Fixtures were installed and the project completed.

To date, the owners have done all of the design and construction work themselves, partly because of a limited budget. Since they were decorating on a budget as well, they decided to experiment with supergraphics as an inexpensive way to add visual interest to a particular wall. The design in the bedroom is a wonderful complement to the curving headboard of the brass bed, and the graphics on the stairwell wall add visual excitement to an otherwise ordinary location.

The owners are planning an extensive kitchen and first floor bath renovation in the near future. The kitchen offers a large amount of existing floor space and the possibility of extension into an enclosable back porch. Despite their own design expertise, they plan to seek professional advice to make the most efficient and attractive use of this critical space.

## 1913 RAVENNA

Eager to preserve undeveloped land for public use within the city, the Seattle Park Board hired J.C. Olmsted, whose father had been the successful planner of Central Park in New York City, to plan a park and boulevard system for Seattle. Olmsted drew a series of connecting parkways that linked existing and planned parks from Seward Park on Lake Washington to Ravenna Park, located north of the University of Washington campus. Much of Olmsted's plan, commissioned and presented in 1903, eventually was implemented by the city, financed in part by four million dollars in bonds sold between 1905 and 1912.

The park system of Seattle made its residential districts even more attractive to prospective homeowners. Parks such as Ravenna, which was acquired by the city in 1911, made adjacent residential development popular with builders as well.

This modest frame cottage, built for a member of the Denny family in 1913, probably served its original owner as a suburban retreat, since it is located just a few hundred yards from Ravenna Park.

The portico of this small cottage gives the facade a deceptively elegant appearance from the street. There are two ways into the house from the entrance porch: through lace-curtained French doors that open into a small dining room, or through the main front door into a large living room. Inside, the house is simple in plan and basic in finish.

The first floor was renovated in 1977 and the current owner bought the house shortly thereafter.

She has furnished the house with a stylish combination of antique and contemporary pieces that enhance each room. For example, the living room combines brightly patterned curtains and a couch with a cobbler's bench, which is used as a coffee table, and several handwoven rugs. A large fireplace is a focal point in this room, especially in the winter when it is used every day.

Sliding pocket doors that once separated the living and dining rooms have been removed and, as a result, the small eating area seems larger than it actually is. Trim around doors, windows, and baseboards has been painted to match the walls. Both living and dining rooms have refinished oak floors. A small built-in corner sideboard holds glassware, silver, and dishes.

The renovated kitchen is a center of activity for this owner who loves to cook. A center island was built to provide more work area. Most of the original kitchen was retained, including existing cabinets and shelves. An unusual feature is a narrow "cool cupboard" built into an outside wall next to the Dutch door that leads to the backyard. This pre-electric refrigerator uses outdoor ventilation to keep perishable foods cool and unspoiled. Although the owner typically uses the cool cupboard to store herbs and spices, she occasionally uses it to store cheese and butter as well.

Although the house has two spacious bedrooms on the first floor, the owner decided to add a guest bedroom and bath in the unfinished attic. She patched cracked plaster, painted the walls, and installed wall-to-wall carpeting over the existing fir floor. A small closet was converted into a bath and paneled in cedar.

79

# 1914 RAVENNA

The present owners of this typical, two-story builder house were attracted to it for many of the same reasons that the original residents must have found it appealing. The house occupies a corner lot two blocks from woodsy Ravenna Park and is filled with characteristic Craftsman-style finish and detail, which have remained in excellent condition since the house was built in 1914. The house was probably a speculative venture for its builder and must have been fairly priced because it sold quickly after it was completed, according to county records. Affordability was also a major consideration for the current owners, who purchased the house in 1967 for $17,000.

The house has remained in good condition largely because it has had only three owners since it was built. Almost all of the original brass light fixtures and switch plates are in place; the original windows, trim, and cabinetry are intact; and the original hardwood flooring in the living and dining rooms is in good condition. Although framed somewhat carelessly, as many builder houses of the day typically were, the house has a basically sound structure and the only major work it has required has been complete electrical rewiring.

The present owners, an architect and his family, have spent countless hours renovating the original structure cosmetically and remodeling certain portions of the house to suit specific needs. Their first task, thirteen years ago, was to clean and lighten the dark interior in the main living areas.

Floor-length draperies immediately were removed to expose large double-hung windows in the living and dining rooms. Wallpaper that had been in place for fifty years was steamed and scraped from the walls. The plaster was in good condition and with light sanding made a satisfactory surface for paint. Finally, slash-grain fir wainscotting and a plate rail in the dining room, and bookcases and other trim in the living room were cleaned to remove the dirt and patina of age.

While they were brightening the interior, the owners also added a small deck just beyond the back door to make the backyard easily accessible and to provide an outdoor eating

area. The deck was the
first evidence of the careful
adaptation of this house to
the lifestyle of its new
owners, a process that has
continued for ten years.

The original kitchen
was in desperate need of
remodeling. It had little
counterspace, worn
linoleum flooring, and
limited natural light. A new
plan simply rearranged
existing space and
eliminated a small butler's
pantry to provide a location
for a large refrigerator. In
addition, a small back porch
was enclosed with French

doors and large windows to create an informal eating area, provide convenient access to the deck, and allow the maximum amount of natural light to enter the entire room.

Although a floor-to-ceiling pantry provided good storage in the original kitchen, the owners created additional storage space by building a series of small open shelves. The existing window above the sink was removed after a small solarium was added along part of the exterior west wall; as a result, both light and air move freely through that opening. An L-shaped cabinet next to the kitchen sink effectively divides the work area from the eating area, and provides additional countertop for food preparation. Oak flooring was installed in the kitchen in keeping with the hardwood throughout the first floor.

The solarium brightens not only the kitchen but also the living room. It serves as a greenhouse, in addition to acting as a light source.

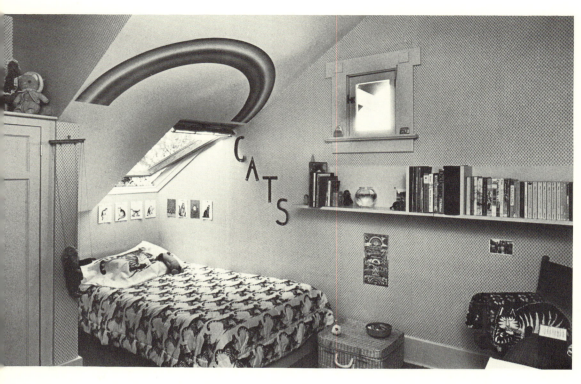

A more recent phase of the renovation is a major bedroom remodeling completed within the last year. There were originally three large bedrooms on the second floor. Since each of the three children wanted a private room, the owners decided to convert the existing space into four bedrooms. By moving walls and incorporating unused attic space, three small bedrooms and a larger one have been created. Two bedrooms have sleeping alcoves tucked under the sloping roofline. All have built-in closets, attractively trimmed and painted to look original. Each room is different, both in floor plan and decor, which adds strong visual interest to the second floor of this house.

The renovation is still in progress. A former garage was converted into a studio-office several years ago and is now rented as a small apartment. A brick terrace has just been finished in the backyard and additional landscaping is being considered. Future plans include a complete renovation of the full-sized basement.

1922 WALLINGFORD

Few building styles were as popular or are as characteristic of Seattle's neighborhood architecture as the bungalow. These small single-story (or apparently single-story) houses, built with a wide variety of materials, appeared on lots throughout the city from 1903 through the late 1920s.

The bungalow style is generally defined by a sloping gable roof and deep porch that extends across much or all of the front of the house. This particular example in Wallingford shows the typical roof, but the characteristic veranda has been reduced to a small covered porch that frames the front door. Regardless of its modesty, this bungalow and hundreds of similar structures offered modern, affordable, and attractive housing to budget-minded Seattle homeowners in locations from Capitol Hill to Ballard during the first two and a half decades of this century.

The Craftsman style, which greatly influenced neighborhood architecture in Seattle between 1900 and 1920, had a major impact on a number of bungalows, including this house. The brackets that support the porch are complemented by exposed roof timbers. Masonry, stone, and, in this case, brick were used for the oversized columns of the porch, and often for sidewalls and railings. In addition, beveled leaded windows, such as the panels above the fixed windows in the living and dining rooms of this house, were common.

Seattle builders and homeowners were so fond of the bungalow style that during the height of its popularity in the 1920s, entire blocks in certain neighborhoods, particularly Wallingford and Green Lake, were built exclusively of bungalows. This house, built in 1922, is one of four very similar houses on the same side of a quiet residential block just south of Wallingford's business district along Forty-fifth Street.

While the exterior appearance of many bungalows varies according to the budget and intentions of the builder, a bungalow interior almost always follows an open plan in which the common rooms are open to one another. This "open" interior, considered very progressive when it was first introduced, quickly became a popular alternative to the separate parlor, dining room, and library design of most Victorian houses, and helped sell the bungalow style to potential owners.

This bungalow features a large living room that extends across the entire width of the house. There is no entry or hallway; visitors simply walk into the central room of the house as soon as they cross the threshold. The living room, which is divided into two separate conversation areas, has a large brick fireplace at one end, flanked by built-in cabinets with leaded-glass doors.

The dining room is separated from the living room by French doors that can be left open; even when closed, they allow visual communication between the two rooms. The kitchen is directly beyond the dining room and features a small breakfast nook and adequate work space.

91

One of the two bedrooms in this bungalow is currently used as a study. The bathroom is located between the sleeping areas. Most bungalows have the common areas lined up on one side of the house and the private rooms on the other. It is a simple, practical arrangement that works very well.

This house has remained in original condition since it was built, only occasionally needing cosmetic maintenance or emergency repair. The current owner considers this residence totally comfortable and practical for one or two adults, much as the original owners must have felt sixty years ago. It is no wonder that the bungalow took Seattle by storm in the 1920s and is still a popular house today.

## 1925 LESCHI

Although some of the seasonal cabins and cottages in Leschi and other lakeside districts were carefully built, most were constructed with little or no regard for quality, either in materials or craftsmanship. Since these structures were intended to be used primarily during the driest and warmest months of the year, builders had little incentive to provide more than basic shelter.

One such house, built as a summer cabin in 1925 and then sold and occupied for thirty years as a year-round rental, was bought by its present owner in 1974. It has become something of a laboratory for his design ideas and painstaking craftsmanship. The owner, an architect, has used his technical knowledge, sense of good design, and almost every minute of his spare time for four years to convert a run-down, almost uninhabitable cabin into an elegant and stylishly hand-crafted small house.

Several practical considerations affected the design and schedule of this complete residential renovation. Budget limitations not only required him to do most of the work himself, but also forced him to use salvaged materials whenever possible. Since he planned to live in the house during construction, it was essential that part of the structure always remain weathertight. He drew plans that would allow completion of the house in stages and immediately went to work.

Although he did not alter the original exterior profile except to convert a small gable roof into a shed, he had to reframe the entire structure to comply with current code requirements. The house had been built with two-by-three inch stud walls and two-by-four inch rafters to support the roof. The structure was not only weak but was also ugly. The sidewalls were covered with asphalt sheet siding, patterned to look like brick. The steeply sloping lot was overgrown with black-berries and weeds.

Once the exterior was reframed and enclosed, the owner decided to concentrate his time, talent, and resources on the interior. He designed a simple, open plan to replace the series of tiny rooms in the original house. The main entry is located at the corner of the basement, which also serves as a workshop. The front door opens onto a steep stairway, adorned by a larger-than-life portrait of a siren from the *Iliad*.

The stairs open into a small landing and hallway that connect the study, bedroom, and bath at one end of the house with the main living area at the other. The living-dining-kitchen area with a sleeping loft above is the center of activity for this house, which because it has only 630 square feet, almost demands such a central area of multiple function.

The entire house is strikingly handcrafted, from the leaded windows and French door panels designed and fabricated by the owner to the mosaic of concrete tile shards that decorates a corner of a small deck just outside the main living area. The owner designed and built every piece of furniture, except the dining room chairs. Custom cabinets with doors and trim of vertical-grain fir were built into the kitchen, bathroom, and living area.

Economy of materials was important in the reconstruction of this house. Durable, relatively inexpensive composition shingles were chosen for the roof instead of costly cedar shingles or shakes. Flooring is one-by-four-inch tongue-and-groove hemlock decking that will eventually be sanded and finished. The owner also saved money by using selected construction-grade fir for interior door, window, and cabinet trim. Once it is carefully sanded and finished, this inexpensive lumber can look much like first quality vertical-grain fir.

99

Landscaping the steep slope both behind and in front of the house has been the final phase of reconstruction. Terraces were constructed of pieces of concrete masonry, salvaged from a local sidewalk improvement project, to prevent erosion and to provide access to the main entry and several decks. With the inclusion of a hot tub, the decks and terraces provide outdoor living and recreation space for much of the year and substantially increase the functional living space of this small house.

# 1926 QUEEN ANNE HILL

No single residential district in the city offers more spectacular views of mountains and water than Queen Anne Hill. The steep south slope with its vista of downtown Seattle and the natural wonders beyond was the preferred location for those early city fathers who wanted to keep a watchful eye on their banks and businesses twenty-four hours a day. Some of the finest houses in the city were constructed by Seattle's wealthiest families on the south and west slopes of Queen Anne, but just blocks away—and often with the same panoramic views—rows of modest, popular houses like those in neighborhoods throughout the city were built.

The houses located closest to the edge of the bluff, which drops sharply to the railroad tracks and commercial activity at Pier Ninety-One and Interbay, have unobstructed views of Bainbridge Island and the Olympics to the west, Blake and Vashon islands to the southwest, and Mount Rainier to the south. There are even a few blocks where houses have northern views of the sound in addition to the vistas to the south and west. On one such block, a formerly undistinguished builder cottage, built in 1925, recently has been renovated into a comfortable and attractive house.

The current owners bought this modest one-and-a-half story frame structure in 1978 and planned extensive remodeling before actually moving into the house. The program they presented to their architect had three major aspects. First, they wanted an outside deck or terrace on the southwest side to entertain or just to relax and enjoy the expansive view. Second, they wanted to renovate the kitchen, which was worn out from decades of use and needed new cabinets, appliances, and flooring. Finally, they wanted to replace the narrow, dark stairway to the second floor and remodel the upstairs into a master suite.

The architect drew plans to accomplish all of these goals and made several other changes in the original structure. The entry was relocated to a more central position and the doorway leading into the living room was blanked out. French doors were installed along the south wall of the living room to provide access to the brick terrace.

The master suite was divided into several zones, with a sleeping area at the top of the new stairwell, a sitting area made possible by a new dormer, and a completely renovated bathroom. The entire second floor is carpeted from wall to wall, the ceiling is paneled in clear-heart redwood, and windows, doorways, and stair rail are trimmed in vertical-grain fir. A spacious window seat was built along the west wall beneath large new windows.

Energy efficiency was a major concern in the remodeling effort as well. A Franklin stove in the upstairs sitting area and a fireplace in the living room are regularly used during the fall and winter. A new pump and boiler were installed in the furnace, extra insulation was put into the walls and roof, and insulated glass was used in new windows and skylights.

In addition, a recirculating fan was installed near the peak of the roof above the stairway to push warm air down from the second to the first floor.

The original living and dining rooms and the downstairs bedrooms were painted and allowed to retain their handsome original coved ceilings, leaded windows, and picture moldings. Despite the contrast in finishes and detail, the first and second floors of this attractive, comfortable house blend quite successfully.

# 1927 CAPITOL HILL

By the 1920s brick had become a popular material for sidewalls and usually served to assure neighbors of the relative prosperity of the owner regardless of the size of the house. This particular two-story brick house is located on the northwest slope of Capitol Hill and is turned ninety degrees from the street in order to fit, albeit snugly, on a smaller-than-standard city lot.

The classic symmetry of the facade that faces the street demonstrates the generally conservative intention of the entire house—a sense of order that carries into the rectangular floor plan. Carefully manicured trees and plantings surround the house in a precise and orderly manner. Inside the house, however, the creativity and hard work of the present and immediately previous owners are apparent, reflected in three substantial remodeling efforts.

Attracted by the central location, the elegant interior details, and the generally spacious feeling, the current owners bought the house in 1975. They planned immediately to remodel the dark and worn-out kitchen, but took a year to think about their goals and expectations, then hired an architect to draw a plan.

Most of the west wall in the original kitchen was removed and replaced with large windows and skylights to allow maximum access for natural light. A new sink and dishwasher were installed under the windows. The room was slightly enlarged by eliminating a wall between a small pantry and the original kitchen.

Custom oak cabinets were installed, with drawers in the base units instead of the usual shelves and doors. Two small stained-glass panels, designed and fabricated by the owners, were mounted as decorative doors on upper cabinets on either side of the sink. A butcher-block table sits in the center of the room and serves as a convenient work space and as an informal eating area. Countertops are tile.

A wood stove sits against a wall across the room and is used to display cookbooks, jars, and kitchen equipment. A six-inch band of wallpaper makes a colorful and distinctive molding along the top of each wall. The original fir flooring was discovered in good condition under several layers of linoleum, and was

sanded and refinished.

The dining room, adjacent to the kitchen, is furnished in handsome country antiques, which give this somewhat formal room a relaxed and lived-in appearance. The addition of stained-glass panels, which the owners made in their basement workshop, to the large fixed window on the wall near the entry, gives the dining room a soft and colorful look. French doors that lead from the dining room to a backyard deck are evidence of the remodeling efforts, which also included substantial renovation of the master bedroom, by previous owners.

The original rectangular plan featured four moderately sized bedrooms and a single bath on the second floor. To enlarge the master bedroom and create a large additional bath, the wall between two bedrooms was removed and a bearing beam put in its place. A large bed and bookcases were built along one wall, and a banquette for reading and relaxing was built under the windows across the room. Two large closets topped with storage cabinets were built and the floor was carpeted. The adjoining bathroom was designed with the sink and vanity in an alcove, and the bathtub and toilet located in a separate room.

The current owners continued their renovation with the conversion of another existing bedroom into a study and sewing room. Although the kitchen had required extensive professional assistance in both design and construction, the new study was their own design and work. The ceiling was opened to expose the attic and roofline. Beams were capped with vertical-grain fir, and several new supports were added. A small stairway to a portion of the attic, now exposed to the rest of the room as a loft, was built through an existing closet. Plywood flooring was nailed across the rafters and a sewing area was created.

In one corner of the room, the owners built a brick hearth and installed a parlor stove. They paneled the ceiling with cedar, installed bookshelves on one wall, and added a comfortable couch. Since the renovation, the room has become an integral part of the house instead of a rarely used guest room.

1928  MOUNT BAKER RIDGE

The popular houses of Seattle's neighborhood architecture often borrowed design elements from fashionable high-style residences, which had been designed and executed by some of the leading architects of the day. One of the most common examples of this practice is the so-called builder-Tudor style, which was in great demand by Seattle home-owners in the 1920s.

Hundreds of modest houses, built in the Tudor style, can be found in Seattle neighborhoods from Montlake to Magnolia, from Laurelhurst to West Seattle. Typically, a builder-Tudor has a steeply pitched gable roof, brick or stucco sidewalls, and an arched opening at the front door-way. Many offer attractive interior detail, from coved ceilings to leaded windows. Hardwood floors are often used throughout the house, and built-in bookcases and other cabinetry frequently are included.

Structural ornamentation with small dormers and turrets is not uncommon, but few builder-Tudors demonstrate the fanciful facade found on this Tudor residence in Mount Baker Ridge. The house combines stucco and half-timbered design with shingle sidewalls. The steep gable roof has bands of decorative shingles on each exposed end. The large turret that dominates the house when viewed from the street serves as a playful exaggeration of the Tudor style.

The current owner of this distinctive variation on the builder-Tudor bought the house in 1974 because it offered so much style and character. Although some cosmetic remodeling had been attempted by previous owners, most of the original finish detail remained intact. Mahogany door and window trim had survived the years in good condition. The unusual decorative tile on the fireplace adds a stylish appearance to the large living room. Coved ceilings give an additional indication of the builder's concern for finish quality, and repeat the soft curves of the openings between the living room and dining room, and the living room and main entry.

A large deck had been added across the back of the house to provide a location for a small swimming pool and to eliminate the difficulties of a sharply sloping backyard. Access to the deck was provided by replacing a small window with a sliding glass panel in a dining room wall. That panel also allows access to a pleasant territorial view of the dense landscaping that surrounds the deck.

The kitchen had been refurbished unsuccessfully by previous owners and was in desperate need of attention when the current owner moved into the house. Existing cabinets were removed and a custom-designed group of plastic laminate units was installed. Oak parquet was laid over worn linoleum and finished in natural tones.

The flooring was extended into the adjoining breakfast room, which was converted to a comfortable sitting area with a new couch and low Parsons table. Track lighting, installed to replace a hanging ceiling light fixture, provides a contemporary contrast to the leaded casement windows, built-in corner cupboard, and other traditional details.

A circular stairway, accented by leaded glass windows, winds up the turret to three bedrooms and a bath on the second floor. Small dormers provide alcoves for reading or catching a brief glimpse of Lake Washington through casement windows with leaded panes.

## 1928 QUEEN ANNE HILL

Three eclectic architectural styles—Colonial, Tudor, and Spanish or California mission—became extremely popular with Seattle builders and architects in the 1920s. World War I had fostered patriotic conservatism among the American people, and Seattle residents fell in step with the national trend. Although each of the popular building styles was romantic, none was so exotic in the gray and rainy Pacific Northwest as the Spanish Mission style.

Stucco sidewalls on a Spanish Mission house are usually white or light-colored, doorways and openings are arched, and the low-pitched roof is red

tile. Floor plans vary from a simple one-story four-room structure to a formal two-story four bedroom house with an outdoor patio or covered porch for additional living space.

Wrought iron and other decorative ornamentation are found on the more elegant examples of Spanish Mission style, such as this spacious residence, located on the south slope of Queen Anne Hill.

The house, purchased by its owners in 1975, is located on a large corner lot and commands a magnificent view of Elliott Bay, the downtown commercial district, and surrounding mountains. The view, which is framed in the house by a solarium and large dining room windows on the first floor, and by large windows in the master bedroom on the second floor, was a major attraction for the owners when they decided to buy this house.

The excellent structural condition of the residence also appealed to the present owners. The house had been occupied by the original owner until 1973, and had received little wear from its occupants. The present owners painted and wallpapered each room, refinished the oak floors, and moved into stylish comfort with no major expense or inconvenience.

Specifications for the original plans of this house were passed on to the present owners by the seller. The architect specified the finest finish materials, from Honduras mahogany for trim and cabinetry to fancy tile surfaces in the kitchen and bathrooms. Wrought iron posts were designed for the railing on the stairway to the second floor. These elegant finish materials and the fine craftsmanship with which they were incorporated into the house were a major attraction for the current owners.

121

The attention to authentic Spanish Mission exterior detail is striking, from the terra-cotta tile roof to the tile vents in the attic to the copper downspouts. A decorative shadow window was cut into the stucco on the upper part of the south wall. The arched front doorway was topped with a small balcony and iron fence.

The interior is similarly stylish. Coved ceilings in the living and dining room complement the arched openings between the rooms. A small bay window with leaded panels on either side of the central window admits maximum natural light and provides space for more seating in the relatively small living room. A large fireplace, framed by a mantel supported by small brackets, dominates the opposite wall. Although the window trim is Honduras mahogany, the painted picture molding that runs around the room is probably fir.

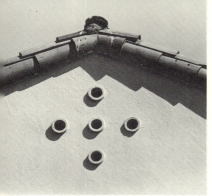

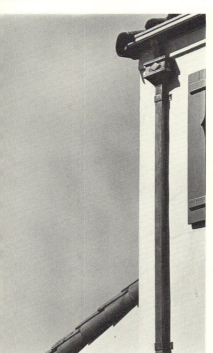

123

There are three bedrooms and two baths on the second floor of this 2100-square-foot house. The master bedroom is actually a suite with a bathroom and separate dressing area. The current owners replaced existing small windows on the south exterior wall with a large three-paneled expanse of glass to frame the panoramic view. Interior shutters were installed over the remaining leaded windows and the room was painted a deep forest green.

The spacious child's bedroom includes a large walk-in closet for maximum convenient storage. Shutters on the windows can be closed for privacy. A third room across the hall is used now as a study.

A large basement currently used for laundry and hobbies may eventually be finished for comfortable use as a playroom. There is also a garage that can be entered through the basement, allowing the owners to escape the rain when parking their car.

# Glossary

| | |
|---|---|
| Banquette | An upholstered bench, often beneath a window |
| Bearing beam | The support on which some or most of the weight of the structure rests |
| Casement | A window sash that opens on hinges fastened to the upright side of the frame |
| Common rooms | Rooms, such as a parlor, living room, and dining room, that are intended for use by the owner and guests |
| Cove | The curved junction between the ceiling and interior wall |
| Dormer | A small gable in a sloped roof, often having a window in the vertical front face |
| Double-hung window | A window with two balanced sashes, one of which slides vertically over the other |
| Eaves | The lower edge or edges of a roof that project over a sidewall |
| Finish | The interior or exterior trim, especially around doors, windows, and stairways; also can include hardware, tile, and other elements of visible *finished* appearance |
| Frame or framing | The skeletal structure of a building |
| Gable | The triangular wall enclosed by the ends of a sloping roof |
| Gable roof | A moderately to steeply sloping roof with gable walls at each end |
| Gambrel roof | A roof with two slopes on each of two sides, with the lower slope steeper than the upper one |
| Hip | The intersection of two roof planes |
| Hip roof | A slightly to moderately sloping roof with two planes |
| Newel | A post that terminates the handrail of a stairway |
| Paver | Quarry, or paving, tile |
| Portico | An entrance porch |
| Prow window | A fixed or casement window with two angled panels of glass, resembling the prow of a ship |
| Ridge | The top horizontal member of a sloping roof into which the rafter ends are nailed |
| Sash | A frame in which glass is set to make a window |
| Shed roof | A roof with a single sloping plane |
| Siding | An exterior wall covering of timber or shingles |
| Wainscot | Wood paneling on the lower part of interior walls |

# Further Reading

*Bungalow Magazine.* Yoho, Judd, editor. Seattle: Craftsman Publishers, 1913–1918. A monthly magazine, edited by Seattle architect Yoho, with plans, specifications, and advice about the bungalow. Intended for developers, builders, and owners of houses in this popular style.

Conran, Terence. *The House Book.* New York: Crown Publishers, 1976. Encyclopedia of styles, plans, practical considerations, and wild ideas. Discusses different rooms, from hallways to kitchens, in detail. Heavily illustrated with color photos and drawings. *The Kitchen Book* and *The Bed and Bath Book* by the same author are excellent sequels.

Gault, Lila, and Weiss, Jeffrey. *Small Houses.* New York: Warner Books, 1980. Ideas from sixteen houses under 1200 square feet in color photos, plans, and text. Houses are located coast to coast; some are new, others renovated or restored.

Hotton, Peter. *So You Want to Fix Up an Old House.* Boston: Little, Brown and Company, 1979. Detailed instructions for doing-it-yourself, from foundation to trim. Good diagrams and drawings, helpful glossary and bibliography.

Owen, John. "Evolution of the Popular House in Seattle." Master's thesis, University of Washington, 1975. This thesis explores the social and economic aspects of Seattle's neighborhood architecture, and gives a thorough discussion of basic architectural style.

Poppeliers, John, Ed. *What Style Is It?* Washington, D.C.: Preservation Press, 1977. Basic guide to major architectural styles in American building from colonial days to the present. Photos and text reprinted in pamphlet form from Historic Preservation series of magazine articles.

Sale, Roger. *Seattle: Past to Present.* Seattle: University of Washington Press, 1976. A scholarly, very readable history of Seattle that combines descriptive profiles of the city's neighborhoods, important citizens, and other colorful text with political and economic growth of the city.

Steinbrueck, Victor. *Seattle Cityscape.* Seattle: University of Washington Press, 1962. A personal perspective on Seattle's architectural profile with special attention to the broad variety of residential and commercial styles found in the city. Includes a visual narrative in pen-and-ink drawings, as well as interpretive text.

————. *Seattle Cityscape #2.* Seattle: University of Washington Press, 1973. More visual and verbal commentary on Seattle's architecture by the city's premier voice for architectural appreciation and preservation.

Stickley, Gustav. *Craftsman Homes.* New York: Dover Publications, 1979. Selected articles from *The Craftsman,* a monthly magazine devoted to the American Arts and Crafts Movement. Numerous prints of Craftsman-style interiors and exteriors, essays on the Craftsman ideal, and other interesting observations.

*Time-Life Encyclopedia of Home Repair and Improvements.* Alexandria, Virginia: Time-Life Books, 1978. Seventeen-volume series including Basic Wiring, Weatherproofing, Adding On, and so on. Heavily illustrated, very practical text. What *Foods of the World* is to the student cook, this series is to the self-taught builder.

*An Urban Resource Inventory for Seattle.* Seattle: Historic Seattle Preservation and Development Authority, 1975. Nineteen city neighborhood profiles in maps, photos, and text. All aspects of urban design are included, but residential architecture is a primary focus.

Vila, Bob. *This Old House.* Boston: Little, Brown and Company, 1980. Print companion to the PBS television series of the same name. Two hundred sixty color photos and one hundred line drawings. Step-by-step instructions on renovation, from appraisal through completion.

Weiss, Jeffrey, and Wise, Herbert. *Living Places.* New York: Quick Fox, 1976. Ninety-six pages of beautiful color photos of diverse and visually appealing interiors. Useful to idea-seekers involved in innovative remodeling as well as in new construction.

Wise, Herbert. *Rooms With a View.* New York: Quick Fox, 1978. More color photos of interiors, shot on location from Boston to Santa Fe, and from New York to Seattle.

Yoho, Judd. *The Bungalow Craftsman.* Seattle: Craftsman Publishers, 1913. A typical book of stock house plans, drawn and published by a Seattle architect. Offers numerous variations of the basic style to builders and owners for a nominal fee.

# Other Books from Pacific Search Press